Contents

Bucket Betcha

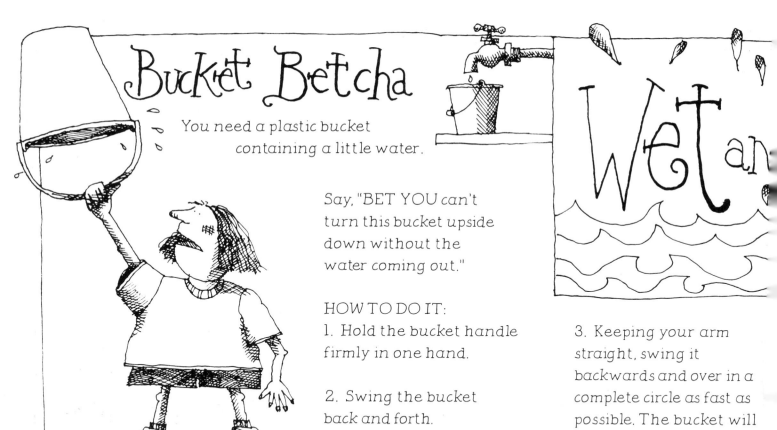

You need a plastic bucket containing a little water.

Say, "BET YOU can't turn this bucket upside down without the water coming out."

HOW TO DO IT:
1. Hold the bucket handle firmly in one hand.

2. Swing the bucket back and forth.

3. Keeping your arm straight, swing it backwards and over in a complete circle as fast as possible. The bucket will go upside down, but no water will come out!

Splosh Racing

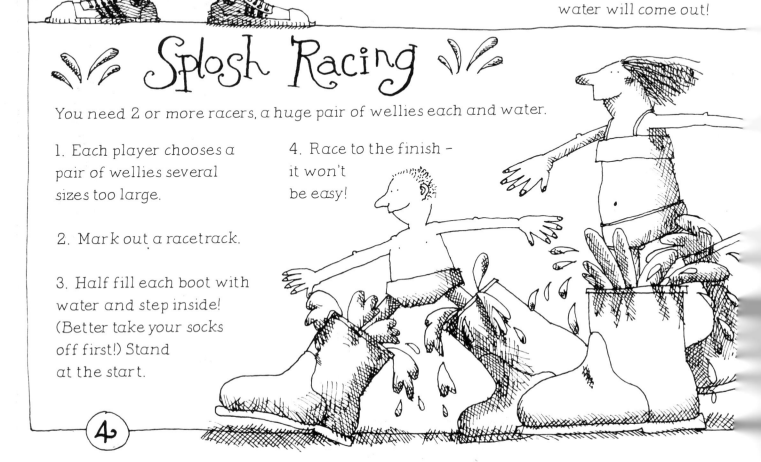

You need 2 or more racers, a huge pair of wellies each and water.

1. Each player chooses a pair of wellies several sizes too large.

2. Mark out a racetrack.

3. Half fill each boot with water and step inside! (Better take your socks off first!) Stand at the start.

4. Race to the finish – it won't be easy!

Wicked

Old King Can

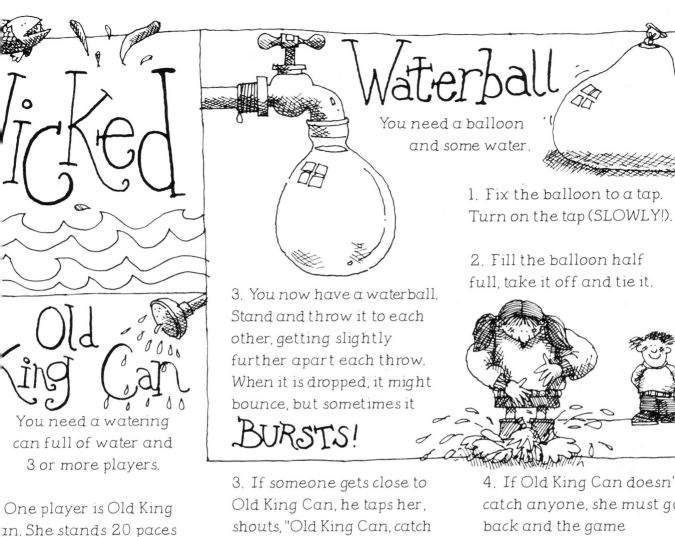

You need a watering can full of water and 3 or more players.

One player is Old King Can. She stands 20 paces away from the other players with her back to them. She holds the watering can.

Everybody creeps towards Old King Can. Whenever she whirls round, everybody stands still. If anyone is caught moving, they must come to stand by Old King Can and she sprinkles them with water. They return to the start line.

Waterball

You need a balloon and some water.

1. Fix the balloon to a tap. Turn on the tap (SLOWLY!).

2. Fill the balloon half full, take it off and tie it.

3. You now have a waterball. Stand and throw it to each other, getting slightly further apart each throw. When it is dropped, it might bounce, but sometimes it **BURSTS!**

3. If someone gets close to Old King Can, he taps her, shouts, "Old King Can, catch me if you can!" and runs towards the start. She chases him. If she manages to sprinkle him, he becomes Old King Can.

4. If Old King Can doesn't catch anyone, she must go back and the game starts again.

5

Hares and Hounds

You need a big bag of twigs.

1. One person (the Hare!) runs off, carrying the bag filled with twigs.

2. She leaves twig arrows as she runs, to show the way.

3. The Hounds count to 100, then set off after her. Gather up the twigs as you run, so you can use them again.

4. The person who catches the Hare wins and takes the bag for the next chase.

5. If you are a particularly cunning Hare, you could set false arrows to fool the Hounds!

Hunts a

Magpie Madness

You need a piece of paper, a pencil and a plastic carrier bag for each player.

1. Make a list of 10 things which might be found nearby (like a daisy, a crisp bag, a snail shell). Some should be easy, some difficult. Each player writes them all down.

2. Set a time limit. Race to find as many things as possible. Put the things in your bag for proof.

3. The winner is the first to collect all the things. If nobody manages this, count up everybody's totals to decide the winner.

hases

for 2 or more players.

The Triffic Treasure Trail

You need some paper, a pen and some treasure (a wrapped present).

1. Hide the treasure.

2. Draw a picture which gives a clue to where the treasure is.

3. Hide this piece of paper somewhere else.

4. Draw another picture which gives a clue to this second hiding place.

5. Hide this too. Carry on until you have a whole trail of hidden clues.

6. Give the last piece of paper to the Treasure Hunters and set them on their way!

Pooh Sticks

You need 2 or more racers, a footbridge over a stream or river and some small sticks.

1. Each player chooses a stick. Stand on the bridge facing upstream. Drop your sticks at the same time into the water.

2. Run across to the other side and wait. The first stick to reappear from under the bridge is the winner.

3. The first person to win 3 times is Pooh Sticks Champion!

Monster Chopsticks

You need 2 or more players, and 2 bamboo poles about 1 m long, a bucket and some medium-sized stones each.

1. At the count of 3, race to get all your stones into your bucket using the poles as chopsticks. You mustn't touch the stones or the bucket with your hands.

2. If you get really skilled, you could race to take the stones out of the bucket too!

Stick Bust

for two o

Jumbo

You need 2 or more play

1. Scatter the sticks higgledy-piggledy into a big criss-crossed pile.

2. Take turns trying to pull sticks out of the pile without moving any oth stick. If you manage it, have another turn.

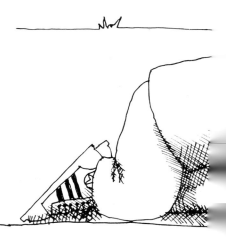

KY NESS

ore sticklers!

ickersticks

a big pile of sticks.

3. The winner is the player with the most sticks at the end.

Skittle Sticks

You need 2 or more players, a handkerchief (or sock), a ball, some string, 9 long sticks and a low branch.

1. Wrap the ball in the handkerchief and tie this to the piece of string.

2. Tie the string to a low branch so that it hangs freely.

3. A little to one side, push the sticks into the ground in a grid shape. Push them in gently so that they are easy to knock over.

4. Check that the ball can swing out past the furthest stick.

5. Swing the ball as shown. Aim to knock over as many sticks as possible in 2 goes.

6. Score a point for every stick knocked down, but 15 points if you get them all in one go!

7. The first player to score 30 points wins.

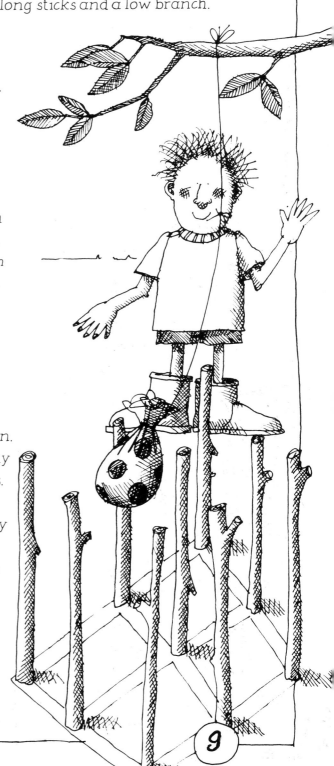

9

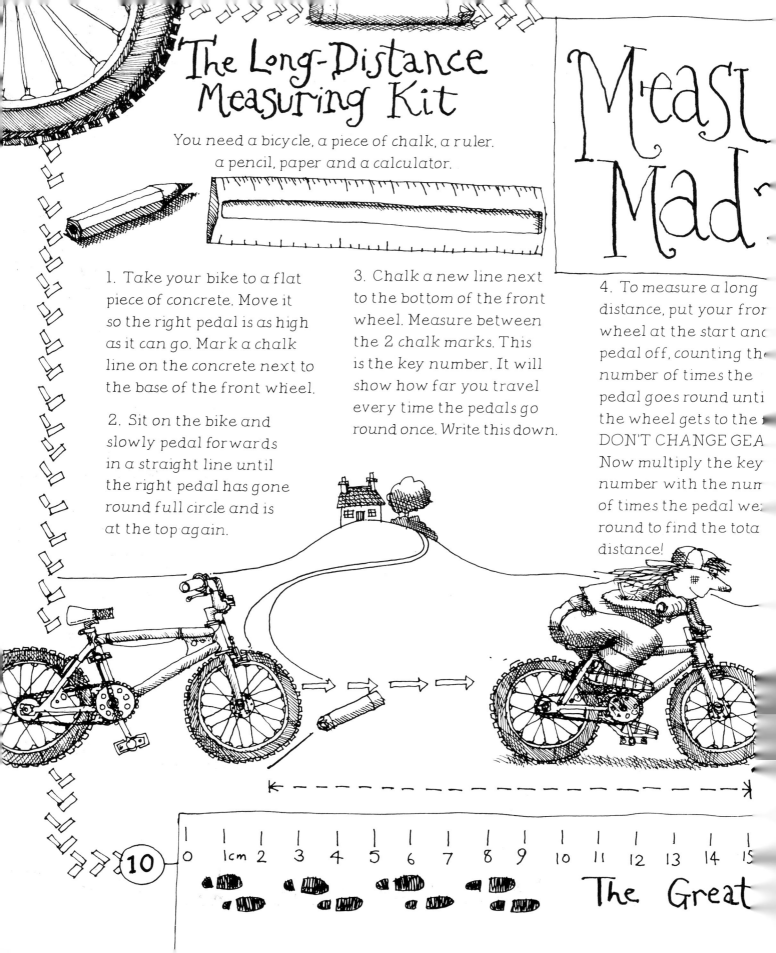

The Long-Distance Measuring Kit

You need a bicycle, a piece of chalk, a ruler, a pencil, paper and a calculator.

1. Take your bike to a flat piece of concrete. Move it so the right pedal is as high as it can go. Mark a chalk line on the concrete next to the base of the front wheel.

2. Sit on the bike and slowly pedal forwards in a straight line until the right pedal has gone round full circle and is at the top again.

3. Chalk a new line next to the bottom of the front wheel. Measure between the 2 chalk marks. This is the key number. It will show how far you travel every time the pedals go round once. Write this down.

4. To measure a long distance, put your fron wheel at the start and pedal off, counting the number of times the pedal goes round unti the wheel gets to the DON'T CHANGE GEA Now multiply the key number with the num of times the pedal wer round to find the tota distance!

| 0 | 1cm | 2 | 3 | 4 | 5 | 6 | 7 | 8 | 9 | 10 | 11 | 12 | 13 | 14 | 15 |

The Great

ement
ss I

The Short-Distance Measuring Kit

You need your feet, the Great Shoe Ruler, a pen, paper and a calculator.

Thunderstorm Distance

To measure the distance of a thunderstorm you need a steady count!

1. When you see lightning flash, start counting, "1 silly second, 2 silly seconds, 3 silly seconds" and so on at a slow even pace...

2. Stop counting when you hear the thunder roll. The number of silly seconds you've counted is the number of miles away the storm is.
(P.S. 1 mile = 1.6 km)

1 silly second, 2 silly seconds, 3 silly seconds...

1. Measure your shoe against the Great Shoe Ruler at the bottom of the page. Note this down.

2. Walk along the distance you want to measure, slotting one foot after another and counting how many steps you take.

3. When you get to the end, multiply your number of steps with the length of your shoe. This will give you the distance you want!

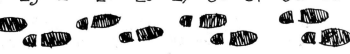

| | | | | | | | | | | | | | | | | |
19 20 21 22 23 24 25 26 27 28 29 30 31 32 33 34

oe Ruler

Dead Letter Boxes

Dead Letter Boxes (DLBs) are places where spies hide messages. A DLB might be under dustbins or stones, in cracks in walls, pinned under benches or buried under flowerbeds. Put your spy messages in jars or small plastic bags to protect them.

Spies an

Dead Letter Game

You need 2 teams of spies, 2 pencils and 2 sheets of paper.

Tom
Mary
John
Sally
Ben

1. Each team lists their names on their sheet of paper.

2. Secretly, each team hides their sheet of paper in a DLB outside.

3. When the game begins, each team hunts for their enemies' DLB. When they find it, they must catch their enemies in the order written on the list.

4. Their enemies must carry on hunting the D while being chased. Cau spies sit down.

5. When one spy team h caught all the enemy s they have won the gam

Signals

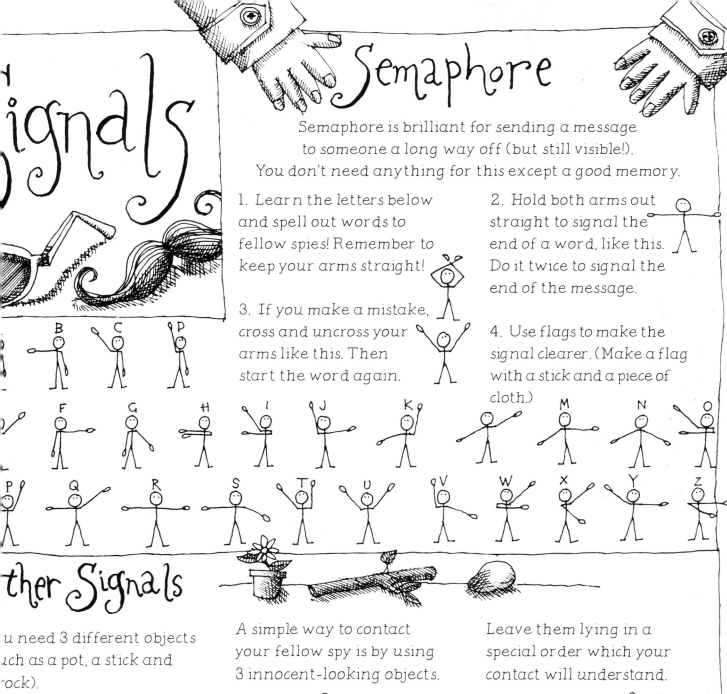

Semaphore

Semaphore is brilliant for sending a message to someone a long way off (but still visible!). You don't need anything for this except a good memory.

1. Learn the letters below and spell out words to fellow spies! Remember to keep your arms straight!

2. Hold both arms out straight to signal the end of a word, like this. Do it twice to signal the end of the message.

3. If you make a mistake, cross and uncross your arms like this. Then start the word again.

4. Use flags to make the signal clearer. (Make a flag with a stick and a piece of cloth.)

B C P

F G H I J K M N O

P Q R S T U V W X Y Z

Other Signals

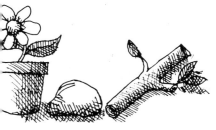

You need 3 different objects (such as a pot, a stick and a rock).

Pot on left = Find me at once!

A simple way to contact your fellow spy is by using 3 innocent-looking objects.

Pot in middle = Message at DLB.

Leave them lying in a special order which your contact will understand.

Pot on right = Danger – enemy nearby!

Animal Parachute

You need a square scarf (silk or cotton), 2 m of string, scissors, an elastic band and a small soft toy. The larger the scarf compared to the toy, the better the parachute will be!

1. Cut the string in half. Hold the pieces alongside each other and tie their middles together.

2. Make a slip-knot on each of the loose ends. Pull 2 of the ends through the elastic band so that it hangs loosely around the middle.

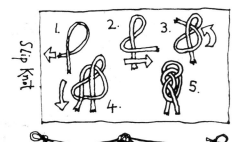

3. Tie knots in the 4 corners of the handkerchief.

4. Slip the ends of the string over each cloth knot and pull to tighten. You now have a parachute!

5. Strap the elastic band round the toy's middle, tucking in under the arms. Roll the parachute up behind its back, like a rucksack.

6. Throw it up as high as you can, or drop it out of an upstairs window and watch it float down!

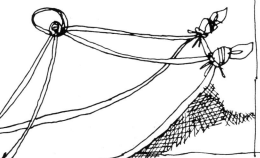

Thing Fly

Incredibl

You need a sheet of stiff thin cardboard, a pencil, a ruler, scissors and sticky tape.

1. Take the cardboard and mark out the lines shown in the picture using your pencil and ruler.

2. Cut out the 3 pieces, a, b and c.

3. Stack pieces a, b and c and tape them firmly together.

4. Practise throwing it in the garden. Throw it like a Frisbee, letting go with a sharp flick of the wrist.

5. Keep practising until you can make it come back!

That

oomerang

30cm

15cm

4cm

4cm

4cm

20cm

The Astounding Microcopter

You need a strip of thin card 26 cm x 6 cm, some coins, scissors, sticky tape, a ruler and a pencil.

1. Fold the long sides of the strip of card in half. Draw a line along the middle of one half. Cut along this line. Fold the 2 halves in opposite directions. These are the rotary blades!

2. Tape a large coin to the bottom of the strip.

3. Throw the microcopter as far and high into the air as you can and watch it spin.

4. Try making a smaller one from a piece 13 cm x 3 cm and use a small coin to weight it.

Super-Kwick Tent

You need a washing line, a large sheet and some weights (stones or earth-filled plastic bags).

1. Lower the washing line so the middle is about the height of your waist.

2. Pass the sheet over the line. Adjust the line's height until about 40 cm of sheet is touching the ground on either side.

3. Pull the sheet out on both sides and hold the edges down with the weights. Hey presto! – a tent!

Tepee

You need at least 5 one-metre bamboo poles, a large elastic band, a large sheet and some string.

1. Stack the poles together into a thick column.

2. Pull the elastic band over the top so it surrounds every pole.

3. Pull out the base of each pole to create a cone-shaped framework.

4. Either drape the sheet over the top, or wrap it round the frame and tie it to the top of the cone.

5. Use the sheet corner, folded back, as the tepee entrance.

ng Camp

Totem Pole

You need some card, some large cardboard boxes, poster paints, a paintbrush, glue or sticky tape and some scissors.

1. First design your totem.

2. Paint the boxes to your design.

3. To add wings (or arms or horns), cut them out on pieces of thin card. Squeeze the wings into slits cut in the box sides.

4. Glue or tape the boxes together in a tower shape.

Igloo

You need a washing line, string, a large sheet, a large cardboard box and some weights (stones or earth-filled plastic bags).

1. Lower the washing line so the middle is about your waist height.

2. Put the sheet out flat under the line, pick it up by the middle and tie this round the line.

3. Pull out the 4 sheet corners to make a square base and hold the edges down with weights.

4. Push the box under the sheet on one side to make the igloo tunnel entrance. Open the base and top flaps of the box to make 2 sets of doors.

Secret Tapper

You need a washer, a drawing pin and
a piece of thread at least 3 m long.

1. Pass the thread through
the washer. Tie the washer
to the thread about 30 cm
from one end.

3. Still holding the thread,
hide behind something a
little way off, like a bush
or dustbin.

4. Wait till someone comes
into the room. Pull and
relax the thread several
times gently so that the
washer taps the window. 3
or 4 taps should be enough
to baffle them!

2. Pin the thread onto the
frame above a window,
so that when the thread
is slackened, the washer
hits the window.

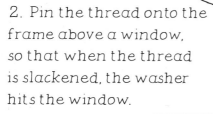

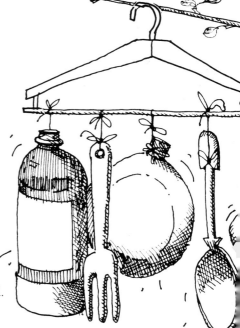

Wind Chimes

You need an old wooden
clothes hanger, string,
cutlery and plastic bottles.

1. Hang the hanger from
a branch or beam so that
it balances.

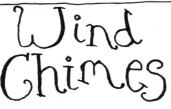

3. Hang them on pieces of
string tied to the hanger.
Balance it by pushing the
looped string back and
forth along the wood.
Make sure they only
touch when moved gently.

2. Find 5 or 6 things which
chime when gently struck
together.

4. Leave them to the wind.

Off!

Washing Line Percussion

You need a washing line, string, plastic bottles, pans, metal and wooden spoons, a large cardboard box and a dustbin.

1. Lower the middle of the line to head height.

2. Hang a range of things from the line using the string. You could try bottles filled with different amounts of water; saucepans, spoons and forks.

3. Experiment with the spoons to find which is the best percussion stick.

4. Use a cardboard box or plastic dustbin for a deep-bass box drum. A metal dustbin could be a kettledrum.

Spoke Clippers

Wind the strip round the fork and thread it through the spokes. Move the wheel slowly. See how long the card needs to be to against the spokes firmly.

You need a bicycle, a strip of hard thin card 20 cm x 6 cm, sticky tape and scissors.

2. Cut the card to make it the right length. Stick it in place round the fork with the tape, as firmly as you can.

Bears and Squares

Outdoor fun is possible even
when walking down a street.
Imagine a large hairy bear is walking
right behind you. If your foot touches
any of the lines or *cracks* between the
paving slabs – he POUNCES! Walk
carefully, or, if you feel bold,
shut your eyes while you jump or
hop forwards. Keep to the squares!
If you touch a line, run as hard as
you can for 10 strides to escape –
but don't land on a *crack*, or
you'll have to run 10 more!

First published in 1993 by Walker Books Ltd
87 Vauxhall Walk, London SE11 5HJ
This edition published 2007
2 4 6 8 10 9 7 5 3
©1993 Alan Snow
The right of Alan Snow to be identified as author of this work has been
asserted by him in accordance with the Copyright, Designs and Patents Act 1988.
Printed in China
All rights reserved
British Library Cataloguing in Publication Data: a catalogue record
for this book is available from the British Library
ISBN 978-1-4063-0637-8
www.walkerbooks.co.uk